ZEN STORIES

AND

PAINTINGS

Published by Brolga Publishing Pty Ltd
PO Box 12544 A'Beckett St Melbourne Australia 8006
ABN 46 063 962 443
email: sales@brolgapublishing.com.au
web: www.brolgapublishing.com.au

National Library of Australia Cataloguing-in-Publication entry
ISBN 9781921596988
Printed in China
Cover design by David Khan
Typesetting by Takiri Nia

ZEN STORIES AND PAINTINGS

STEPHEN CASSETTARI

www.stephencassettari.com

'TO MY FATHER
WHO BREATHES
HIS WAY.'

PART ONE

Pebbles on the Road

The stories and saying in this book are a combination of my original work and adaptations of traditional and contemporary sources. The sayings marked ★ and all the paintings are my original work. The saying on the page preceding the introduction is inspired by the work of Guillaume Apollinaire. I have rewritten the traditional stories to unify the style but whatever their source they all point directly to the heart, clearing away the unessential and leaving only that which *is*.

Pebbles on the road...
    Dancing in the rain...
Swimming between the islands...
    Skipping over the canyons...
Playing among the stars...*

'Go to the edge,' the voice said.
'No!' they said. 'We will fall.'
'Go to the edge,' the voice said.
'No!' they said. 'We will be
pushed over.'
'Go to the edge,' the voice said.
So they went...
    and they were pushed...
      and they flew...

Introduction

PEBBLES OF THE ROAD IS A COLLECTION OF parables, sayings and paintings that portray the spontaneous immediacy of Zen.

Zen is a school of Buddhism which advocates sudden enlightenment or awareness as apposed to the more gradual evolution of the other meditative schools of Buddhism. One of its methods of conveying the essence of understanding is through the use of parables, sayings and universal images of nature.

Zen if often used separately as a term to indicate that which is immediate. Here! Now! This is the interpretation of it in this book.

The text and illustrations are used together in this book because in the Oriental approach, words and pictures cannot be separated as they are part of each other — the words compliment the picture and the sentiment is made clear. In their simplicity the ink paintings transcend words.

To allow the reader to come to their own understanding of this book the parables included are written with open endings and the sayings can be interpreted on a variety of levels. Some can reveal deeper, even opposite meanings from their surface interpretation, present the essence of each event.

Thus, the anecdotes, sayings and paintings enhance each other and present a concept of awareness to be absorbed, but also leave enough unstated for the reader to arrive at their own understanding.

All the concepts in this book engender a quality of strength and hope to encourage those on the road of daily existence.

LOOKING IN
THE LIGHT

A MAN CAME HOME LATE AT NIGHT, AS HE WAS approaching his gate he took the house key out of his pocket. In doing so he accidentally dropped I on the ground where it was lost in the darkness.

He walked up to the door, which he found his wife had left ajar for him. He turned on the hall light and began to search around the floor, looking under the furniture for his missing key.

His wife, awakened by the light and noise, came downstairs and asked him what he was looking for. When re replied that he had lost his door key she too got down on the floor and began to search.

The man turned on the lights of the living room and continued to search. After some time of fruitless searching his wife asked him exactly where he had dropped the key. When he replied that he had lost it at the gate, she stood up and demanded to know why he was looking for it in the house. He calmly replied that it was far too dark outside and there was much more light inside the house.

A candle in the dark
    seems bright
until it meets
    the sunlight.

Freedom is not the liberty
    to do what you want.
Rather it is the ability
    to do what is required.

GIVING THE MOON

A MONK SITTING ON THE VERANDAH OF HIS house was absorbed in the contemplation of the full moon. A thief entered the back of his house and began to search for valuables. The monk heard a noise and went inside to investigate. When he saw what the thief was doing he said to him, 'Let me help you,' and proceeded to load the thief up with valuables. He then showed him out the front door and once again took up his position on the verandah. Looking up at the moon he said to himself, 'I can give you everything I have but I can't give you the moon.'

Later that night some soldiers brought the thief back to the monk's house. They told the monk they had caught him in possession of the monk's goods. 'He did not steal them,' said the monk. 'I gave them to him.'

The soldiers then went away leaving the thief with the monk. The thief, amazed at the monk's generosity, sat down on the verandah beside him and looked up into the sky to see what the monk was so absorbed with.

'Now,' said the monk. 'I can give you the moon.'

Some steal my money
    others steal my time.
But if I feel no remorse,
    they commit no crime

'Neither giving nor taking,
    nothing is gained or lost.
Offering and accepting,
    everything is worth the cost.'

SAILING ON THE RIVER

A GREAT CHINESE LANDSCAPE ARTIST SPENT many months on a large mural. Having completed the final strokes he stepped back to survey the finished work. He sighed deeply and told his apprentice that his was his greatest work and that he could never hop to do a better painting.

He handed his brush to his apprentice and walked up to the edge of the mural. He then calmly stepped onto a rock painting in the foreground of the mural and got into a boat that was moored beside it. He raised the sail and steered the boat across the lake where he rounded the headland and disappeared forever beyond the horizon.

Living on the edge
      is perilous,
   but the view more
         than compensates.*

The act of painting
      is like walking on water.
If you think about
      what you are doing
         you fall in.*

MAYBE

A FARMER LIVED JUST OUTSIDE A SMALL village at the base of some hills. He had a fine son who was much admired by his neighbours. When the neighbours would compliment the farmer on his good fortune in having such a son, he would shrug his shoulders and quietly say, 'Maybe it's good fortune, maybe it's not.'

One day the farmer's stallion broke out of its field and ran off into the hills. When the neighbours came to console the farmer on his bad fortune, he simply shrugged his shoulders and said, 'Maybe it's bad fortune, maybe it's not.'

The son went to look for the stallion and found it at the head of a herd of twenty wild horses. When he led his father's stallion home the other horses followed it into the field. The neighbours came to congratulate the farmer on his good fortune at such an addition to his stock. The farmer replied, 'Maybe it is, maybe it's not.'

When the son was breaking in one of the wild horses it threw him and he landed hard on the ground and broke his leg. The neighbours came to offer their condolences to the farmer. 'How unlucky!' they said. 'Maybe,' said the farmer.

The next day a messenger from the emperor brought a decree to the village conscripting all able-bodied young men into the army. Because of his injury the farmer's son was not conscripted.

Accept neither success
nor failure.*

A circle begins anywhere. *

HEAVEN AND HELL

A GREAT AND POWERFUL WARRIOR CAME TO the head monk of a monastery. He asked the monk to show him the difference between heaven and hell.

The monk sneered at the warrior and said, 'One as arrogant and small-minded as you would never be able to learn the difference between heaven and hell.' After more such abuse the warrior lost his temper and yelled, 'I will show you death then!' and began to draw his sword out of its scabbard.

The monk smiled widely and calmly said, 'That is hell.' The warrior at once understood and pushed his sword back down into its scabbard.

Again, the monk smiled and said, 'And that is heaven.'

If you climb
on a tigers back
the difficulty
is in getting off again.

A long journey reveals
the strength of a horse.

HERE ALL THE TIME

A MOTHER AND HER YOUNG SON WENT TO THE busy market place and became separated. After frantically searching for her son throughout the market his mother finally found him playing beside a stall that sold toys.

'Weren't you worried when you got lost?' cried his mother. The boy replied, 'I was not lost, I was here all the time.'

Never hope
and do not worry.

When you see
a man drowning
you do not wait
until he calls for help
before you rescue him.
Though it is advisable
to ensure that he is
not merely waving
to a friend.

THE OBSTACLE

AT THE END OF A HARD DAY'S WORK, A farmer left his hillside field and began descending the narrow, winding path to his home. He carried his spade and hoe and his dog followed him.

Along the path the farmer found that a fallen rock was blocking his way. Tired and hungry, with dusk approaching, he began digging at the base of the rock to attempt to move it. After much struggle he still couldn't move it and he felt even more tired.

The dog, having wandered away, came back and barked at the farmer. The dog tried to lead the farmer away from the rock, but he was determined not to be distracted from his objective and continued in his struggle.

Again the dog tried to get the farmer's attention but the farmer ignored him. Because it was getting dark the farmer decided to stay where he was and sleep in the hollow he had dug.

Upon awakening in the early morning light, he heard his dog barking further along the path, beyond the rock. After taking a few steps back from the rock the farmer could see that, having been so close to the rock in his efforts to move it, he had not noticed that the fall of the rock had made a rough passage to a lower section of the path.

The water is not impeded
by the rock,
but flows effortlessly
round it
wearing it away with time.*

The falling rock is not deflected
from its path,
but parts the water,
leaving it to continue
on its own journey.*

THE ROSE AND
THE OAK

AN OAK TREE GREW IN A GARDEN FOR MORE than forty years. One summer a nearby rosebud began to unfold the glorious colours of its petals. The oak tree was tired of being the same dull shades of green and brown and longed to be as beautiful as the rose. One morning, when the rose was in its full glory, the tree told the rose of its desire to be like it. The rose in turn expressed its admiration for the height and strength of the oak to change places for a day. And so with the aid of the garden spirits, they did.

That afternoon a gardener came and cut the rose to take into the house.

After the rain –
Everything grows
more beautiful.

flowers do not explain
their beauty.
The storm gives no reason
for its anger.*

THE DRAGON'S EYES

A MASTER ARTIST WAS REQUESTED TO APPEAR at the emperor's palace to paint a dragon mural for the emperor. He replied that he was too busy on more important work and he would not be able to paint the mural.

The emperor's secretary called on the master artist with a royal command for the artist to appear at the palace to pain the mural. Again the artist replied that he was too busy.

The emperor's personal guard came and took the artist by force to the palace and told him he must paint the mural or be executed. The artist proceeded to pain a most magnificent dragon of blue and green, embellished with gold. He worked without stopping and finished the mural in a single day.

The emperor's secretary came to view the completed mural and declared it a great work of art. He paid the artist the amount of gold decreed by the emperor and said that the emperor would view the mural with the court the following morning.

The artists stayed to put the finishing touches on the mural. When all the palace was asleep he mixed white paint with ground pearl and placed a small dot in the centre of each of the dragon's eyes. Gathering up his paints and brushes he then departed for the distant mountains.

The next morning the mural was unveiled before the assembled court. Just as praise was being given for the life-like quality of the work the dragon's eyes blinked. The dragon then turned his head around, stretched his wings and flew out of a palace window, leaving a blank wall that bore only the read seal of the artist.

I walk among beggars and kings
  without being noticed.
But I don't mind
  it leaves more time
    for sunsets and children.*

A shadow has no shadow.

LESS AND LESS

THERE WAS A FARMER WHO WAS ALWAYS looking for ways to save his money. He sold his horse to buy a smaller, less expensive donkey, making it do the same amount of work. He also decided to save even more money by feeding it less.

He reduced the bale of hay he fed the donkey by a handful each day. It was so little, that he thought the donkey would not notice. Eventually, the donkey was performing the same amount of work on less than a quarter of a bale of hay and the farmer was very pleased with himself.

The farmer was very surprised and most upset when one morning the donkey was found dead in its stall.

One stone at a time.

You can't step
in the same river twice.

TWO MONKS

TWO MONKS WERE WALKING BACK TO THEIR monastery when they came to a ford at a stream. At the ford a pretty farmer's daughter asked them to help her to cross the stream as she did not want to get mud on her new dress.

The first monk ignored her and continued on his way remembering the strict rules of their order not even to look at women. Without speaking the second monk picked her up in his arms and carried her across the stream. He let her down on the other side and continued walking with the other monk.

The first monk began to chastise him, asking him if he had forgotten about the strict rules of their order. He kept referring to the incident all the way back to the monastery.

As they reached the gateway of the monastery he referred to the matter again. The second monk turned to him and said, 'Are you still carrying the woman with you? I left her at the stream.'

When you have finished
eating your rice
wash out your bowl.

The illusion of choice
leaves only disappointment.
The joy of acceptance
offers understanding.*

STOP CRYING

A MAN OF LEARNING CAME TO THE HEAD MONK of a monastery to ask about the nature of the monastery's teaching.

He asked the head monk many questions, which were in fact statements of what the man believed the teachings were about. To all his statements the head monk listened calmly, gently nodding his head and replying, 'Yes, that is so.'

Finally the man said, 'Then you have nothing to tell me as I already know what you teach.'

'Oh no,' replied the monk. 'The teachings are nothing like you believe them to be.'

'Then why have you been agreeing with me?' demanded the man.

The monk smiled kindly and replied, 'Before you can feed the baby you must stop it crying.'

Before an action,
hesitate.
During the action
do not hesitate.

Emptiness is full
of potential.*

THE TRUE STUDENT

A LEARNED MONK HAD MANY STUDENTS WHO lived in a temple with him. One student used to steal from the others. After many appeals to their master to reprimand this student, the other students presented themselves before the master with the ultimatum that either he dismissed the thief or they would leave.

The master bowed and replied, 'Then you must go, for you are all good students and will easily find another to teach you but this thief is irredeemable and if I throw him out he will find no-one else to care for him.'

Do not confuse truth
with sincerity.

Mountains are higher
than rivers.
But each follows
its own course
under the sky.*

THE FULL CUP

AN ARROGANT BUSINESS MAN CAME TO A monastery and said to the head monk, 'I have learnt much of the material world in my life so far. Now I wish to learn of spiritual knowledge.'

The monk said, 'Maybe you will get the opportunity but first let us have a cup of tea while we discuss this matter.'

After making the tea the monk poured some into a cup, set for the business man. When the level of the tea reached the top of the cup the monk kept on pouring and it overflowed onto the clothes of the business man. He jumped up and exclaimed, 'What are you doing?'

The monk replied, 'You are like the cup, so full that there is no room to put in any more. First you must empty yourself.'

You have begun
once the intention
is there.

All you need to be rich
is treasure in your heart.*

THE THREE BROTHERS

A RICH MAN WAS DYING SO HE CALLED HIS three sons and said to them, 'I wish to leave my fortune intact so I will set each of you the same task to see which one is the most capable at managing money.

'In my warehouse there are three large storerooms, all of the same size. Here is a bag of silver each. Your task is to each fill one storeroom with as much as your silver will buy.'

The first son bought sand with all his money and filled a third of his room.

The second son bought soil with all his money and filled his room.

The third son spent only a small portion of his money and bought some candles and matches to fill his room with light.

Quality
rather than quantity.

Intuition is spontaneous knowledge
gained through experience.*

THE IMAGE OF THE DRAGON

THE IMAGE OF THE DRAGON IS OFTEN SEEN in the expressions of nature; in the vapours of the clouds, the flowing of water or fire, twisted tree trunks and eccentrically shaped rocks.

The Chinese dragon has no wings and breathes no fire; it swims through the air by the undulations of its body like an eel in water. It produces fire by the friction of its body movement against the air.

It is an auspicious symbol, bringing good luck to those who see it, clearing away illusion and revealing truth.

The depiction of the five-clawed dragon was the prerogative of the emperor. The four-clawed dragon was for lesser officials and the three-clawed variety for more common use.

The dragon consists of the head of a horse, the horns of a deer, the man of a lion, the body of a snake and the feet of an eagle.

Being large one has
     respect for the small.
Being old one has
     sympathy with the young.*

Cherish carefully
     the friendship of nature.
Let her gracious blessings
     fill your quiet moments.

EXERCISES IN BEING

Think — Understand.

Wait — Passively alert.

Eat — According to need.

Look at the stars.

Talk to a rock.

Hug a tree.

Listen to the rain.

When in company
act as if alone.

When alone act as if
in company.

Spend one day without speaking.

Spend one hour with eyes closed.

With eyes closed,
have someone you are close to
take you on a walk.

Think of something to say
to someone particular.
next time you see them,
don't say it.

Go somewhere in particular
to do something.
When you get there
don't do it.

Walk backwards.

Upon awakening
immediately get up.

Get dressed to go somewhere
then don't go.

Just go out immediately
as you are, anywhere.

Do what comes next.

Walk on!

SEEING THE LIGHT

LIGHT A CANDLE,
observe the flame.
Close your eyes,
and still see the flame.
Watch as it slowly fades.
look at the flame again.
Light another candle
from the first flame.
Nothing is taken away
from the first flame.
Let the two flames
merge together.
Is there one flame or two?
Blow out the flame.
Where did it return to?
With eyes closed
see the image of the flame.
Blow that out too.
What is left…?★

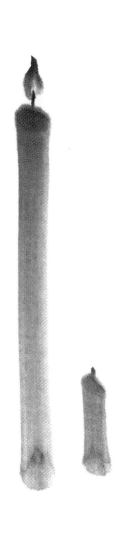

PART TWO

Reflections on the River

Laughing in the rain...
Singing with the waterfall...
Reflections on the river...
Waves upon the shore...
Sailing over the ocean...
Drifting amid the clouds...*

Distance is covered
   by being still.
Change is achieved
   while remaining.
Heights are overcome
   by descending.
Understanding is revealed
   by admitting ignorance.*

INTRODUCTION

Reflections on the River continues the main concept from
my first book on Zen sayings, Pebbles on the Road. The
concept is that the journey of life is not a complex mystery
but rather a revelation of the simple path we can take it
we choose to. Just as the way of the river is to follow the
most natural course on its journey to the ocean, we too can
follow this course if we keep things simple.

    The stories I have written are developed from
traditional oriental sources. They express the idea of
direct experience: when a bend is turned in the river, a
different view is revealed and a glimpse of new perception
is acquired. These glimpses develop into a continuous
rhythmic flow of experience that can pervade even the
most mundane daily acts in our lives. The changes or 'bends'
in life may seem difficult at first but they are the very things
that guide us on our way.

    The stories are complemented by the sayings which
are rendered in gracious calligraphy. They contain visual
harmony as well as simplicity. That which is essential is
further refined in the ink paintings which transcend words.

    Together, the art of poetry, calligraphy and painting
present a unified concept of being. In this way traditional
understanding is conveyed and retained so that obstacles on
the river of life become merely indications of the direction
to the ocean.

SWEEP THE FLOOR

A MAN SEEKING WISDOM CAME TO A MASTER who lived in the city and asked him if he would take him on as a student. 'I do not teach,' said the master. But after much inquiry, the master a greed to take the man on for one year.

The master began his teaching by saying to the man, 'Before study of spiritual matters one must be competent in everyday concerns. Your first instructions are to sweep the floor of the house each day. Then you may spend the rest of the day as you please.'

After three months of meticulously performing this task the man asked the master if he could begin his lessons. 'First you must help in the kitchen by doing the washing up,' the master told him. This task took him half the day.

When another three months had passed the man once again approached the master, asking to begin his lessons. 'Very well,' replied the master, 'but first you must help in the garden'. The man found this task took him all day and left him with little time or energy to do anything else.

Finally, after another three months the man confronted the master in exasperation and threatened that if the master did not begin his lessons immediately, he would leave. The master patiently told the man, 'You have already absorbed all the lessons and you are indeed ready to leave. There is no more you need to learn from me.'

Don't jump to conclusions.
The rock you thought you
    were going to land on,
    could just be a puddle of mud.*

Your resolutions are as strong
as the company you keep.*

ALMOST FINISHED

THE ITINERANT MONK, NAY-LEE, SAT FOR seven days contemplating the winding river below the cliff. The head man of a nearby village was aroused by curiosity and came to inquire into the purpose of the monk's meditations. The head man was followed by a dozen villagers. 'I have come to build a place of peace for all the people of the village,' answered Nay-Lee.

'When will you begin this project?' asked the head man.

'I have almost finished it,' responded Nay-Lee, 'but I will need you worthy people to complete the job'. As he said this Nay-Lee pointed to the flat area of ground behind him where a few stones seemed to be placed at random. One close observation the villagers could see that the seemingly random stones were in fact markers for the positions of walls for a building.

Desire comes before action.*

It does not matter how long
you can stay under water,
but whether you are still alive
when you come up.*

WHAT IS IMPORTANT

AN ELDERLY ABBOT REALISED HE WAS CLOSE to the end of his life and so gathered all the people of his monastery together, to tell them of his departure and to choose a successor. He asked each person in turn how they would act as abbot after his death.

A very long serving monk told the abbot he would continue the abbot's teachings exactly as the abbot would have done himself. A bolder monk said he would keep the abbot's basic principles but also introduce some newer approaches. Another monk replied that he would change much of the abbot's teaching principles to suit the changing times. The abbot proceeded down the line of those assembled and continued to received answers that put emphasis on the teaching procedure and principles.

At the end of the line stood a young farm girl who had recently been admitted into the monastery. Her job was to help in the kitchen. When the abbot asked her what she would do if she was in charge she replied, 'First I would sweep out this courtyard, it's filthy'.

She got the job.

It's not how you look
but what you see.*

It is the mud of daily existence
    that feeds the roots
      of the spiritual flower.*

FOLLOWING THE MASTER

TWO CHESS MASTERS SAT DISCUSSING A GAME they had just finished. They were playing over variations stemming from one particular move that white had made in the opening. An onlooker interjected, 'You should not have played that move, it is not recommended in the book on this opening theory.'

'My dear Sir,' replied the master, 'I can play this move if I want to. After all I wrote the book you just mentioned.'

Often the best thing to say
is nothing.

The impossible is
what no one can do,
until someone does it.

TROUBLES

A LEARNED MAN TRAVELLED FAR FROM THE city to a monastery in the mountains, to sit before an honoured monk. 'Your wisdom and advice are well-known' said the learned man. 'I have studied the scripture diligently and have meditated arduously. Now I seek to deepen my spiritual understanding without the distraction of the city as I still have difficulty making progress.'

The monk scratched his balding head and said, 'You think you have troubles! My wife is always nagging me for a better house and my daughter needs money to go to college.'

Answers to the question,
    'What is Zen?'...
The river flows amid
    the canyons
    where gnarled pine trees grow.*

In the morning birds sing
    and play amid the bamboo.
In the evening fireflies
    are seen on the hillside.*

NOT LOST

A LORD BECAME SEPARATED FROM THE REST of his hunting party and wandered onto a forest path. He came to a humble straw cottage and saw an old farmer sitting inside.

The farmer had come to visit his son who lived in the cottage. The lord stopped his horse and looked haughtily down at the farmer. 'Which is the way back to the city,' he yelled demandingly at the farmer.

'I don't know,' puffed the farmer, not even looking up from his pipe.

'Which way to the nearest town then?' snapped the lord.

'I don't know,' was again the reply.

'You useless rag of a man,' said the lord. 'Don't you know anything?'

'I know I'm not lost,' murmured the farmer as he nodded off into a restful sleep.

Having no shoes
seems a blessing
when meeting a person
with no feet.*

If you take yourself lighter
the world becomes brighter.*

THE BEST TEACHER

A CLASS OF ADVANCED STUDENTS HAD A GREAT teacher who made every lesson absorbing and easy to learn. There seemed to be no limit to the extent of her knowledge.

After one interesting class some of the students remarked among themselves that to fully appreciate each lesson they should do extra study. They agreed to enrol in an evening course on the subject.

When they arrived to take their places in the evening class they were suprised to see their regular teacher in the classroom. They assumed she was to be their evening class teacher. They were even more surprised when another teacher entered the room and began to teach. Their own teacher took a seat among the students and listened to the lecture while diligently taking notes.

When the teacher is ready
the student appears.*

I know nothing
and I am not even sure of that!

SHOW ME

A MONK CAME TO HIS ABBOT AND SAID, 'I HAVE meditated now for many months but cannot concentrate on the precept you have given me. My mind keeps distracting me with other thoughts. How can I keep my mind focused?'

'Well,' said the abbot, 'show me your mind and I will see what I can do for you'.

'There isn't anything I can show you,' replied the monk.

'Well is there isn't anything there, how can it bother you?' concluded the abbot.

All things must pass.

Even when no eye can see
and no fragrance
can be perceived,
the flowers still blossom.

WIND AND SUN

THE WIND WAS ROMPING AROUND THE SKY boasting to the sun how mighty it was. 'I can tear down trees and buildings and cause storms and trouble everywhere,' bragged the wind.

'Then show me some of this power,' said the sun.

'See that traveller down there scurrying along the road with his cloak tight around his shoulders? Well take his coat away from him if you are so powerful.'

'Ha!' shrieked the wind. 'Such an easy task for one of my strength. It will only take a moment.'

The wind then hurtled to earth to perform his dare.

At the first tug of wind the monk wrapped his cloak tight around his body and plodded on. As the wind tore around him gripping at any loose corner he grimly held his cloak even tighter for warmth.

Angry that one mere person could defy him, the wind raged down on the traveller who finally had to seek shelter among some overhanging rocks. He continued to hold onto his cloak. With one last gust of wind that nearly swept the traveller off his feet, the wind departed in disgust. Roaring up the sky the wind scoffed at the sun, 'I'd like to see you do any better with such a stubborn person as that!'

The sun smiled and beamed warmth down onto the rocks and the traveller cautiously came out and resumed his journey. As the sun grew even warmer the traveller unhooked his cloak and carried it under his arm. Plodding on in the increasing heat and weary from his struggle with the wind, the traveller became very tired. He found a grassy place in the shade of a tree and laid down to sleep, leaving the cloak unattended beside him.

Anger is like a wild horse:
 before you mount
   decide if you can handle it.

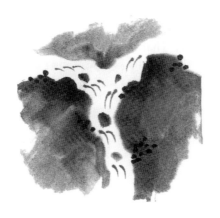

The tighter you squeeze water
 the less you can hold.*

MIRACLES

AN ASCETIC WHO LIVED CLOSE TO A VILLAGE wanted to impress the village people with his power. He practised for many years, following a strict regime, to gain the skill to walk on water.

After many years he gathered the people of the village on the shores of a nearby lake. As they watched he calmly walked out over the surface of the water and then returned to shore.

While he was recovering from this rather strenuous effort the head of the village came up to him and said, 'That was impressive but some of us are wondering why you didn't just learn to swim'.

When the question is,
   "How much?'
The answer is always,
   'Just enough.'*

Horse and tiger
   drink from the same stream.*

JUSTICE

Nay-Lee, the monk of Moon Mountain, was renowned for his fair and wise decisions in matters of dispute between the people of the village on the river. Two farmers came before him concerning a dispute. Both of them claimed ownership of a particularly fine laying hen, which had wandered from one farm to the other.

'Are you certain that this is your chicken?' asked Nay-Lee. Both farmers pleaded earnestly that the hen was their property. 'Very well,' said Nay-Lee. 'You both seem like honest fellows so I believe you both. Therefore I will divide the chicken equally between you.' As soon as he had spoken Nay-Lee picked up the hatchet and raised over his head to cut the hen in half.

Just as he was about to smite the chicken one of the farmers screamed out, 'Wait! I may be a chicken thief but I will not have you kill such a fine bird as this.'

Turn fear into anger
   and anger into laughter.*

A stranger is
   a friend with whom
you have not
   yet become acquainted.

FROM THE HEART

AYOUNG ARTIST WALKED ACROSS A MOUNTAIN slope, looking for inspiration for his next painting. After many hours of walking he came across an old man sitting on a rock. The old man was sketching with a piece of burnt wood onto a pad resting on his knees.

When the young artist approached the old man he saw he had drawn a small hut beside a lake. The drawing was sketched quickly but was so full of life that one expected the hut door to open and its occupants to appear. The artist looked at the view and saw a deep valley and trees swathed in mist.

Once the old man had paused in his work the young artist asked him why he drew this scene when he was surrounded by quite a different view.

'Ah!' exclaimed the old man as his breathed heavily. 'It is only what is in the heart that can be given expression. Not what is in the eye.'

Living in the mountains –
the sound of birds.
Close to the river –
the sight of fish.*

The quietest calmest
place in the world,
is right inside of you.*

DOING WHAT IS BEST

A FARMER AND HIS SON WERE WORKING IN their field which was beside the road to a town. It was a hot day and as the son had left his straw hat at home, the farmer gave his hat to the boy to wear.

Two travellers passed by and the farmer overheard one of them remark to the other, 'Look at that young boy wearing a hat while his poor father suffers under the sun. Has he no respect for his elders?' The farmer, who hoped he had taught his son respect, took the hat off his son's head and wore it himself.

Later he overheard two passing farmers, 'Look at that man so strong and fine, wearing that hat to protect himself while his fragile youngster has to endure the sun's rays'. So the farmer took the hat off his head and once again placed it on his sons head.

Later still the farmer heard two women comment on the poor farmer suffering in the heat while his son remained comfortable. Determined not to have to listen to any more such remarks, the farmer took the hat and cut it in half, placing half on his head and half on his sons head.

'Look how silly those two look,' came the remarks, as the farmer and his son worked on in the field

Don't change horses
mid-stream.

Don't wait for tomorrow
to arrive before today
has departed.
Leave yesterday
where you found it.*

THREE WISHES

ONE DAY A WOODCUTTER WAS WALKING through the forest when he heard shrill cries. Following them he found a wood gnome trapped under a fallen tree.

'Help me!' cried the gnome.

'Why should I?' replied the woodcutter, for he knew the tricks of wood gnomes well.

'Help me and I will grant you three wishes,' pleaded the gnome.

Knowing wood gnomes to be mischievous but also true to their word, the woodcutter lifted the fallen tree off the gnome. The gnome thanked him and scurried off saying, 'There is no hurry to use the wishes, just use them wisely'. The woodcutter rushed home to tell his wife of his good fortune.

His wife, on hearing the news, berated him.

'You will surely waste these wishes just as you have wasted your life,' she screamed.

She continued her tirade for some time until the woodcutter became so impatient he snapped back at her. 'I wish you weren't here then I could think clearly how to use these wishes.' In a flash his wife vanished. The woodcutter was horrified at this because he really loved his wife deeply. At least I can put things right thought the woodcutter. He said aloud, 'I wish for my wife to be returned to me.'

Instantly she reappeared, hardly having paused for breath and continued to harass him. 'Look what you have done,' she scolded him. 'You have already wasted two wishes.'

The woodcutter sighed in despair and said, 'Oh I wish I never had any wishes'.

You can only get there
from here.*

Before you can find
the solution
you must know
the problem.*

ONE OR MANY

A GROUP OF STUDENTS WERE TRAINING UNDER an aging warrior. One morning, after giving them some exercises to practise in his courtyard, the warrior went inside his house to clean his weapons. After a short time the students began to disagree among themselves over some points of the exercise. Some of them even came to blows.

On hearing the noise, the warrior returned to the courtyard and the students separated at his presence. 'Bring me a bundle of twigs from the wood cellar' said the warrior to a student. The student returned with a bundle of twigs which were tied together at both ends so they were easy to carry.

'You who are so full of energy!' the warrior commanded. 'Which one of you can break this bundle with your bare hands?' Some of the stronger students tried to break the bundle but to no avail.

'It can't be done!' they exclaimed.

'Well that depends on your point of view,' said the warrior as he untied the bundle and snapped the twigs one at a time until they all lay broken in front of him. 'If you quarrel among yourselves you will be easily defeated, but if you band together you will be invincible!'

True strength is not resistant
but resilient.*

Teach the student
not the subject.*

Images of water

The clouds, so large,
are not heavy.
They float
high above the earth.

The rain falling
on the trees,
drips from the leaves
in a cascade of sound.

The stream
washes over the rocks,
finding a path
down a hillside.

The river spreads wide
to both banks.
Boats drift on their way
to destinations.

The lake reflects
the rising moon.
Fish play
among the reeds.

The ocean waves
lap a receding shore.
The vast expanse
is calm and deep.

The mist rises
where the sea meets the sky.
Clouds return
over the shore.

Harmony of
complementary opposites

BALANCE IN THE UNIVERSE IN MAINTAINED BY two inseparable opposites: Yin and Yang.
These opposites combine to create and maintain harmonious accord around a moving centre; just as light and dark revolve around a day.

The two can become one and this one is greater than the separate pair. They become one just as male and female can create new life. This new life also harmonises with its opposite to create more life. In zen this is the true meaning of rebirth and eternal life.

The most well-known symbol that expresses the traditional concept of harmonious balance of Yin and Yang is that of the Tai Chi (Grand Ultimate). There are many other symbols that also express this concept such as the one below.

In this symbol the interplay of the fluid natural world is shown in harmonious accord with the more stylized world of humans. Together the two complementary opposites form one complete unity that brings into being many forms.

Complementary opposites of Yin and Yang are portrayed in the basic elements of nature. These are described on the pages opposite.

IMAGES OF NATURE

Water
Tranquil reflection pool
Surging ocean waves

Fire
Comforting wood glow
Raging forest destruction

Earth
Tender growing grass
Earthquake chasm

Wind
Soothing summer breeze
Furious hurricane*

Exercises in being II

Breath – Fully.

See - Deeply.

Listen – Carefully.

For no reason – Smile.

Bake some bread.

Hold a baby.

Listen to a fire.

Walk barefoot a little each day.

In the rain, wear no hat
and keep your head up.

For five minutes follow
the path of an ant.

Grow a plant from a seed.

Make up the words
and sing a song.

Let your feet dance
as they will

Occasionally, stand on your
head, using a wall for support.

Each day be still in a moment
and absorb five different sounds.

Each evening recall
one new event that happened
to you during the day.

Cry a little.

Laugh a lot.

Walk on!

VOYAGE

FAR FAR AWAY TONIGHT,
    far from this distant land.
    Out where the stars are bright
and white foam flowers are found.

There I'll steer my ship
for no distant harbour shore.
But I'll set her sails for horizons,
evermore.

Where a timeless sun
shines on a silver sea.
While the never silent waves,
dance softly around me.

And though I'll be alone
far out on the water.
I'll drift through endless days,
held gently by heavens daughter.

O mother of life,
hold me in your arms.
Lull me with the music
of your waves
and I shall find peace,
in the depths of your heart.

Where does the ocean go?*

The End

		QTY
Zen Stories and Paintings	$19.99	....
Postage within Australia (1 book)	$5.00	....
Postage within Australia (2 or more books)	$9.00	....

TOTAL* $_____

* All prices include GST

Name: ....

Address: ....

....

Phone: ....

Email Address: ....

Payment:

❏ Money Order ❏ Cheque ❏ Amex ❏ MasterCard ❏ Visa

Cardholder's Name:...

Credit Card Number: ....

Signature:..

Expiry Date: ....

Allow 21 days for delivery.

Payment to: Brolga Publishing (ABN: 46 063 962 443)
             PO Box 12544
             A'Beckett Street, Melbourne, 8006
             Victoria, Australia
             admin@brolgapublishing.com.au

Be Published

Publishing through a successful Australian publisher. Brolga provides:

- Editorial appraisal
- Cover design
- Typesetting
- Printing
- Author promotion
- National book trade distribution, including sales, marketing and distribution through Macmillan Australia.

For details and inquiries, contact:
Brolga Publishing Pty Ltd
PO Box 12544
A'Beckett St VIC 8006

Phone: 03 9600 4982
admin@brolgapublishing.com.au
markzocchi@brolgapublishing.com.au
ABN: 46 063 962 443